JOB BASICS™
GETTING THE JOB YOU NEED

GETTING A JOB IN
HEALTH CARE

CORONA BREZINA

ROSEN
PUBLISHING®

NEW YORK

Published in 2014 by The Rosen Publishing Group, Inc.
29 East 21st Street, New York, NY 10010

Library of Congress Cataloging-in-Publication Data

Brezina, Corona.
Getting a job in health care/Corona Brezina.—First edition.
    pages cm.—(Job basics, getting the job you need)
Includes bibliographical references and index.
ISBN 978-1-4488-9610-3 (library binding)
1. Medical personnel—Vocational guidance. 2. Allied health personnel—Vocational guidance. I. Title.
R690.B658 2014
610.69—dc23

                                                                    2012047069

Manufactured in the United States of America

CPSIA Compliance Information: Batch #S13YA: For further information, contact Rosen Publishing, New York, New York, at 1-800-237-9932.

CONTENTS

INTRODUCTION   4

Chapter One   SURVEYING THE FIELD OF HEALTH CARE   7

Chapter Two   YOUR HEALTH CARE EDUCATION   22

Chapter Three SEARCHING FOR HEALTH CARE JOBS   34

Chapter Four   PREPARING FOR TESTING AND
                   JOB INTERVIEWS   44

Chapter Five   ACING YOUR JOB INTERVIEW   52

Chapter Six   THE FIRST DAY OF YOUR NEW CAREER   62

                   GLOSSARY   69

                   FOR MORE INFORMATION   71

                   FOR FURTHER READING   74

                   BIBLIOGRAPHY   76

                   INDEX   77

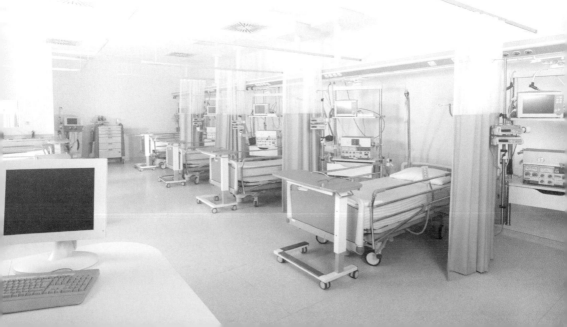

INTRODUCTION

A young nursing aide arrives early at the hospital and checks in to work. She's wearing a crisp uniform that still looks almost brand new It's a big day for her. After intensive on-the-job training, she's finally going to start her regular duties.

The job is an important responsibility. A nursing aide provides the most basic medical care for patients in health care facilities. He or she is the caregiver that patients turn to first. A patient might tell the nursing aide about a health concern. The aide will relay the concern to a nurse or doctor. If it requires treatment, the aide may participate by dispensing medication. Aides also attend to patients' day-to-day health, comfort, diet, and hygiene. A nursing aide has more personal contact with the patient than any other member of the medical team.

While she's waiting for the elevator, she thinks for a moment about the high school program that put her on the path to becoming a nursing aide. She had signed up for the allied health program at her local vocational-technical institution. After graduating, she had enrolled in a one-semester nursing aide training course at her nearby community college. She had passed her certification exam after completing the course. It didn't take long to receive a job offer, since nursing aides are in high demand on the job market. She is already thinking about the possibility of taking additional training in

A CAT scan technician examines an image. Medical imaging specialists are in high demand in the job market. Many educational programs in the field take less than two years to complete.

the future so that she can get a more specialized job in occupational therapy.

Can you imagine yourself working as a nursing aide someday? Perhaps you would be interested in a health care job, but your real aptitude lies in technology. You'd want a job that requires computer expertise and an ability to use high-tech equipment. In that case, there are plenty of health care jobs that may pique your interest. For example, health information technologists and medical imaging technicians are also in high demand.

A wealth of information on health care careers is available in the Bureau of Labor Statistics's (BLS) *Occupational Outlook*

Handbook. For each occupation, the *Handbook* outlines what you'd expect to do on the job. It describes the work environment. It details what sort of education, training, and certification are required—many health care jobs require an associate's degree from a community college or less. The *Handbook* lists the pay for the job—many health care workers earn good wages. It also projects the expected job outlook for the next ten years or so—many health care jobs are expected to see faster than average growth in employment. The *Handbook* also lists organizations that can offer more information on each specialty.

The overall economic situation in the United States may be uncertain, but health care industries continue to grow. Many workers appreciate the economic security of a good job in health care. Health care is a promising field for new entrants to the workforce at all levels of education. Entry level workers with an associate's degree or less can enter the field in a variety of specialties. For many young people weighing their options, a health care job could easily provide a secure and rewarding path to success.

CHAPTER ONE

Surveying the Field of Health Care

ealth care is a huge career field. It deals with many different aspects of people's physical and mental well-being. A health care worker can choose from a variety of jobs and job settings. Specialties exist within the field that match just about every personality type and skill set. Are you analytical and exacting? Try looking at health technician jobs. Are you compassionate and eager to help people? You might be a good nursing aide. Are you sociable and a natural problem solver? There might be a good medical assistant position for you.

Thinking About a Health Care Job

Many health professions require high levels of education and specialized skills. Doctors and nurses undergo extensive training for their jobs. But doctors, nurses, and other highly trained specialists are supported by a huge workforce of other health care professionals. Many of these jobs require only an associate's degree, which can be completed in two years or less. Some jobs require even less training. And don't forget that health care workers are in high demand. It is possible for a high school graduate to find a basic health care job immediately upon graduation and complete training on the job.

If you're considering the field of health care, don't be scared away by long job titles! You might see a job title like "electroneuro-diagnostic (END) technologist" and assume that it's way beyond your capabilities. But if you read the description, you'll find that an END technologist is the person who handles certain specialized medical equipment. A community college student can complete an END program in twelve to twenty-four months. Likewise, many other health care jobs with complicated-sounding job titles may be more easily attainable than you might at first believe. In fact, certificate programs for some health care careers can be completed in less than a year.

Don't forget that general medical workers are required in a variety of specialty practices. You might be interested in a specific health care field only to find that it requires a high level of education. Art therapists, for example, treat problems such as mental illness with art, music, and dance. You might think that it sounds like an exciting career

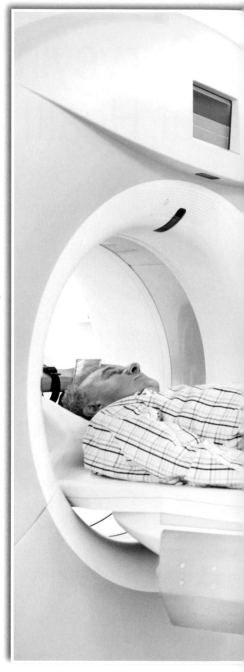

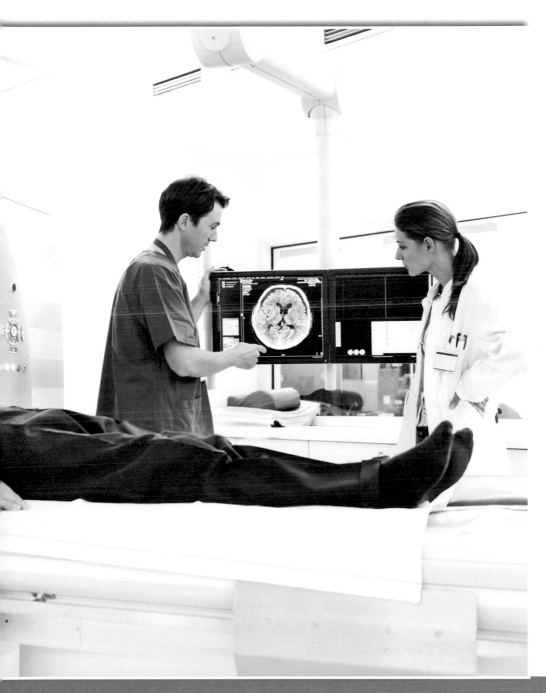

A medical technician assists a doctor during a computed tomography (CT) scan, a powerful tool that produces cross-sectional images of a patient's body.

path, except that it usually requires at least a four-year degree. But an art therapy practice hires employees such as medical assistants in the office. You might pursue a job as a medical assistant with the aim of getting your foot in the door, pursuing more education and training while working, and eventually rising up to gain a position as an art therapist.

Checking Out Your Options

The American Medical Association (AMA)—the leading professional association related to medicine and health—lists nineteen different health career categories. If you're considering different career areas in health care, this list could be a good place to start to zero in on the health care job that best suits your interests, skills, and abilities. Here is a brief description of the AMA's nineteen categories of health care careers:

- Allied health is a catchall term that describes medical professionals other than doctors, nurses, and dentists. Many allied health workers are specialized. They may be experts in a certain type of patient care or medical testing. A number of allied health care jobs—including END technologist, respiratory therapist, surgical technologist, and medical assistant—require an associate's degree or less. If you are interested in becoming a medical technologist or technician, or an assistant or aide, there are a wide variety of career options in allied health areas.
- Communication sciences deal with patients with problems such as speech or hearing difficulties.
- Complementary and alternative medicine and therapies include nonmedical treatments for health issues.

This includes practices such as acupuncture, chiropractic care, and massage therapy. Nonetheless, practitioners in such fields are often highly skilled and educated.

• Counseling is a field related to mental health. Counselors help people work out their issues and achieve personal success.

• Dentistry deals with oral health—people's teeth, gums, and mouths. Dentists are helped by dental hygienists and dental assistants. Dental hygienists perform dental care tasks such as teeth cleaning, patient examinations, and X-rays. Dental assistants assist the dentist during treatments and perform other tasks in the office. Many community colleges offer programs in dental hygiene and dental assisting. A dental assisting program can be completed in under a year.

• Dietetics is the science of food and nutrition. Experts in the field offer advice on designing and following optimum diets for good health.

• Expressive/creative arts therapies use art, music, and dance to treat mental and physical health issues.

• Health information and communication deals with the administrative side of health care. Organizations use medical records and health information technicians to help tend to medical data, increasingly in digital formats. Medical transcriptionists listen to and transcribe dictated material. This means that they produce written records of what a doctor says on a recording. Both occupations require either a certificate or an associate's degree.

• Laboratory science provides the means of diagnosing and treating many illnesses. Highly specialized scientists are assisted by clinical assistants, technicians, and technologists.

A music therapist plays the guitar for an autistic child. Music therapy, either in individual or group sessions, can address a number of physical and psychological treatment needs.

• Medical imaging and radiation therapy are diagnostic and treatment procedures. Machines take high-tech medical images that can be used to determine what's wrong with the patient. Radiologic technologists, for example, take X-rays of patients. Radiation therapy is used to treat patients who have cancer. Some entry-level jobs in medical imaging and radiation therapy require only an associate's degree.

• Medicine: The field of medicine includes a broad range of specialties.

• Nursing is the biggest field within health care. There are more nurses than any other type of health care worker. It generally takes at least three years of education to become a registered nurse (RN). If you're interested in the fundamentals of nursing, however, you may consider pursuing a program to become a licensed practical nurse (LPN), also called a licensed vocational nurse (LVN). LPNs/LVNs work under the direction of RNs and doctors. It takes only a year to complete a LPN/LVN program. Nursing aides, orderlies, and attendants also help perform basic care for patients. These occupations require a certificate or sometimes on-the-job training.

• Pharmacy: Patients go to the pharmacy for prescriptions and information about their medications. Pharmacists are assisted by pharmacy technicians. Many pharmacy technicians receive on-the-job training, although some community colleges offer pharmacy technician programs that generally last less than a year.

• Physician assistants perform many of the same types of duties as a doctor.

• Podiatry is the medical field that involves people's feet. Podiatrists are assisted by trained podiatric assistants.

• Psychology and psychiatry: The field of psychology deals with mental health. It is slightly different from psychiatry, another field that addresses mental health issues. Unlike psychologists, psychiatrists have medical degrees and can prescribe drugs. Psychiatrists are assisted by psychiatric technicians and aides. Technicians, who generally have an associate's degree, help treat patients. Aides, who receive on-the-job training, help with patients' day-to-day welfare.

A physical therapist works with a patient during a rehabilitation session. Physical therapists help patients recover even after medical treatment has ended. They also promote fitness in order to prevent future medical issues.

• Therapy and rehabilitation: Patients sometimes require therapy and rehabilitation to improve their everyday lives if they have been treated for a medical condition or have a disability or chronic illness, either mental or physical. Therapists address a broad range of patients' needs. They are assisted by occupational therapist assistants and physical therapist assistants. Two-year programs for these jobs are offered at community colleges. Occupational therapist aides and physical therapist aides are trained on the job.

• Veterinary medicine: The practice of veterinary medicine is considered a health care field. Veterinarians are assisted by veterinary technicians, who hold associate's degrees. Veterinary assistants and laboratory animal caretakers provide care for animals and help during surgery. They generally receive on-the-job training.

• Vision-related professions include a broad range of occupations, many of them highly specialized. A dispensing optician is one job within the field that is in high demand. Dispensing opticians supply contact lenses and help fit people with glasses. The job generally requires only a high school diploma and an on-the-job training course, although community colleges also offer educational programs.

Do You Have What It Takes?

A career in health care can be intensely satisfying. At the end of the day, you'll be able to say that you made someone's life better. A conscientious health care worker can earn good money and be guaranteed job security. Also, there are many options open to you in health care. As you've seen, health

A doctor helps an elderly patient walk with the aid of a walker. Health care workers interested in caring for seniors might look for jobs in nursing homes or assisted living facilities, where residents live relatively independently.

care includes many different types of jobs. In addition, health care professionals can find work almost anywhere in the country. There are also many possible job settings. If you don't want to work in a hospital, you might look for a job at a medical office or clinic, an outpatient care center, a residential care facility, or a home health care service.

But there are challenges to a health care career, too. Some are practical day-to-day requirements. A job may require hours at a desk or hours on one's feet. Working with patients can be physically demanding—are you capable of supporting a person's body weight while assisting him or her with basic needs? Also, health care doesn't always allow for a nine-to-five schedule. Patients require attention around the clock. Many health care workers work long shifts or put in hours on nights, holidays, and weekends.

GERIATRIC AMERICA

The population of older adults in the United States is rapidly growing. This has implications in the home, the workplace, governmental social policies, and many other areas. It is particularly relevant in the field of health care.

Older Americans require more medical attention than the average population. As a result, there will be an increase in demand for health care workers overall and a particularly high increase for certain specialists. Home health aides will be needed for people who require help with basic care. Occupational therapist and physical therapist aides and assistants will be needed to help people adjust to living with chronic conditions or recuperate from health crises. Long-term care facilities will be hiring more health care workers from many specialties, from nursing aides to psychiatric technicians.

A health care job also requires certain skills and personal qualities. If you work with patients, you must be compassionate and understanding. If you work in a lab or operate medical instruments, you must have good analytical skills. Health care workers in every specialty must pay close attention to details. They also must have good interpersonal skills. Many health care workers are part of a team. You'll be more likely to succeed if you treat your colleagues with respect. Also, technicians, assistants, and aides often have to take direct orders from doctors, nurses, administrators, and other higher-level health care workers. If you're an independent-minded type of person, you will have to come to terms with the idea that you can't talk back or argue with your superior.

Good customer service skills are another positive trait for health care workers. Many jobs, such as dispensing optician, medical assistant, and pharmacy technician, deal directly with customers or patients in a customer service setting. Even for other health care workers, though, basic customer service skills can help make a good impression. Examples include listening, problem solving, a courteous professional attitude, and a positive work ethic.

Starting Out with the Basics

A recent high school graduate might opt for a basic, entry-level health care position. It's a good choice. Experience in a health care workplace can provide a solid foundation for a future career. Even if you decide to pursue other ambitions later on, the skills and knowledge you gain from a health care job may prove useful. And if you do decide to continue in the field of health care, a basic job can be a good starting point for further training or education. When considering applicants to programs related to health care, community colleges look favorably on factors such as health care work experience.

Two examples of basic health care positions are home health aides and medical assistants. Both jobs are in high demand. Both are good places for beginners to gain experience in the health care field.

A home health aide provides health and personal care for individuals who require assistance for medical reasons. A position may be short-term, such as when a patient is recuperating from surgery. Often, though, long-term care is necessary, such as when the patient is elderly or disabled. A home health aide may work for multiple patients at the same time, periodically making scheduled visits at each home. Sometimes, an aide works exclusively for a single patient. Home health aides also work in residential facilities such as nursing homes. Home health aides are supervised by nurses or other medical professionals. They make frequent reports on the patients' progress. Home health aides should be trained in emergency procedures.

Duties for a home health aide include basic medical care such as applying bandages, checking vital signs such as pulse rate and blood pressure, and administering medication. Patients may need help with hygiene, such as bathing and grooming. A home health aide may also perform basic household tasks such as cleaning, cooking, doing laundry, and shopping for groceries. Lastly, a good home health aide should be compassionate and attentive to the patient's emotional and psychological state. Personal care aides, a related occupation, do not perform medical duties.

Medical assistants perform a variety of functions that vary according to job description. They often focus on either

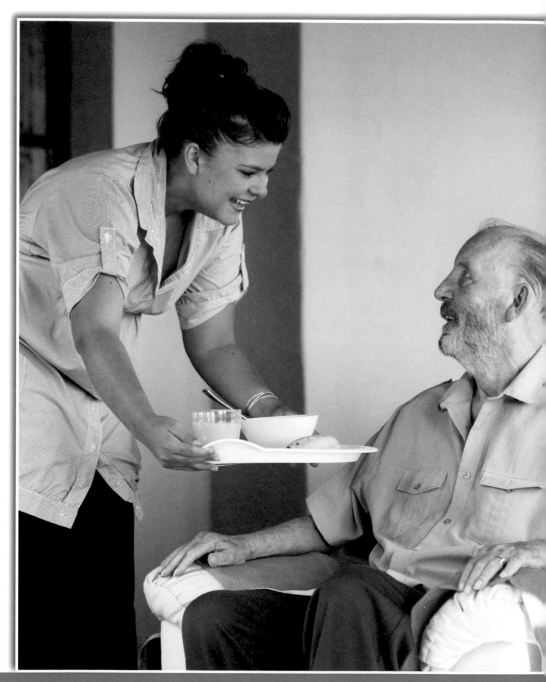

A home health aide brings a meal to a client. Home health aides should be capable of planning healthy meals that address any special dietary needs related to their clients' health conditions.

clinical or administrative work. Some medical assistants work at the reception desk scheduling appointments, answering patients' questions, and performing other office duties. Others work directly with patients. They may review a patient's health history and take vital signs before an appointment with a doctor. They may assist during an examination. Some medical assistants perform basic lab work or help maintain medical instruments. In specialized medical practices, medical assistants are also specialized. A podiatric medical assistant, for example, may take casts of a patient's foot.

CHAPTER TWO

Your Health Care Education

I f you have the ambition to succeed in a health care career, you need to take control of your education. You may have been told that the best path to earning a good living is to earn a bachelor's degree. It's true that a four-year degree is advantageous in the job market, but you should weigh your options carefully. If your instincts tell you that you're not interested in spending four more years in school, you may be right to pursue another educational path. In terms of future job earnings, you are likely to be better off if you complete a training course at a community college than drop out of a four-year course of study without completing a degree. There are many well-paid occupations that require less than a bachelor's degree. In fact, a majority of health care workers possess less than a four-year degree.

It All Starts with High School

This doesn't mean that school isn't important! You need to make good academic choices and strive to acquire the education you need and distinguish yourself while doing so. This starts in high school.

For most health careers, you should take as many high school classes in science and math as you can manage. If your school offers courses in anatomy or health, sign up for them.

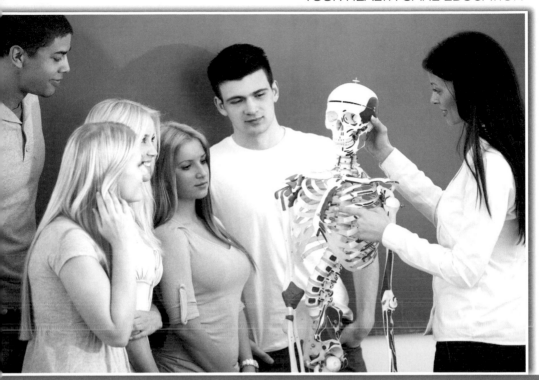

A teacher points out features of the musculoskeletal system on an anatomical model. Students interested in a health care career should take any classes offered on general health or anatomy and physiology.

If you are interested in a career related to mental health, take a psychology class. Also, most jobs require basic computer skills, so you should take classes in computers. Good communication skills are important in most jobs as well, so be sure to take some English classes. Check out specific educational recommendations in guides such as the American Medical Association's *Health Care Careers Directory*.

In addition, you should participate in extracurricular activities that might help your prospects in a health care career. Your school might offer activities such as science clubs or fairs. Some schools facilitate volunteering. If yours does, you might find volunteer opportunities related to health care.

Activities that aren't directly related to health care offer good experiences as well. Participating in sports demonstrates a commitment to fitness and health. Programs such as the debate club hone communication skills and analytical thinking.

An after-school or summer job during high school offers you the opportunity to gain new skills and experiences as well as earn money. It will look good on applications or résumés since it demonstrates that you're able to balance school, work, and personal time. It also shows that you've been able to handle responsibility.

Vo-Tech Programs

Vocational-technical (vo-tech) programs open to high school students offer great opportunities to learn real-world skills during high school. Many graduates of vo-tech programs are able to find jobs in their field directly out of high school. Vo-tech classes can also provide a solid foundation for future college study, either in a community college or a four-year program.

Students in vo-tech programs often attend regular high school academic classes during the morning and spend their afternoons at the vo-tech center. Some vo-tech programs are full-time. Specific programs of study vary from one school to another, but many offer courses related to health care. Some institutions offer a general course in health care, such as "allied health," "biomedical sciences," or "athletic health care" programs. Others offer training for a specific occupation. A few common examples include dental assisting, health information technology, medical assisting, nursing assisting, occupational therapy technician, and pharmacy technician. A

A job as a dental assistant requires both technical skills, such as preparing instruments and equipment, and interpersonal skills, such as interacting with patients and educating them on proper dental care.

vo-tech program may fully prepare students for certification testing in some specialties.

Some vo-tech health programs create partnerships with local colleges and universities. Students may be able to earn college credit in their field while still attending high school at the vo-tech center. Vo-tech programs may also partner with hospitals, giving students the opportunity to complete clinical rotations in a health setting.

Continuing Your Education

You might be tempted to accept a basic health care job straight out of high school instead of continuing with your education. But just a year or two of additional coursework at a community college can make a significant difference in your earnings potential. Even if you take some time off from school after graduating high school, you might want to include further education in your long-term plans.

In the summer of 2012, the BLS issued a report on high-paying jobs that did not require a bachelor's degree. The report included a list of twenty occupations requiring an associate's degree that paid over $50,000. Eight of them were in the field of health care: radiation therapists, nuclear medicine technologists, dental hygienists, registered nurses, diagnostic medical sonographers, radiologic technologists/technicians, respiratory therapists, and occupational therapy assistants.

You can earn an associate's degree at a community college. Community colleges are generally designed to serve students from the surrounding area. They are more easily affordable than four-year institutions. Many admissions offices encourage

ONLINE EDUCATION

Online classes can be an affordable and convenient means of advancing your education. Many community colleges offer some courses online. You may choose to sign up for them as you pursue your certificate or associate's degree. Or you may take one or two classes in order to improve your skill set. There are also colleges that operate exclusively online and provide almost all their instruction on the Internet. Research the institution carefully before you enroll, however. Some of these online colleges make unrealistic claims about graduates' job prospects in their advertisements. You don't want to end up deep in student loan debt but unable to find a job.

students from all academic backgrounds to apply, as long as they're willing to work hard. Night classes may be available in some programs, so you could start to take courses while holding down a job. Community colleges provide a high-quality education that can ensure good career prospects.

In some health care fields, you may have the option of pursuing an associate's degree, certificate, or diploma. The degree program will take longer to complete, but it will provide a more thorough education. A graduate holding an associate's degree will be more competitive in the job market and earn more money. Community colleges also offer postsecondary nondegree awards. These are shorter programs of study that provide a slightly lower level of expertise than an associate's degree. After completion, a student receives a diploma or certificate. Many health care jobs such as assistants and aides require a diploma or certificate.

On-the-Job Training

Many new workers learn the job during a formal training period. An entry-level worker may begin as a helper before working independently. Types of training vary greatly depending on the specific occupation and workplace. Many hospitals provide highly structured, formal on-the-job training. This might take the form of an internship or residency. Hospitals may also pay employees' tuition for continuing education. Pursuing further training, especially in specialized skills, can provide opportunities for advancement. It can be a path to a promotion or a pay raise. Some health care employers provide apprenticeship opportunities in specialties such as nurse assisting. An apprenticeship involves a combination of instruction and hands-on learning.

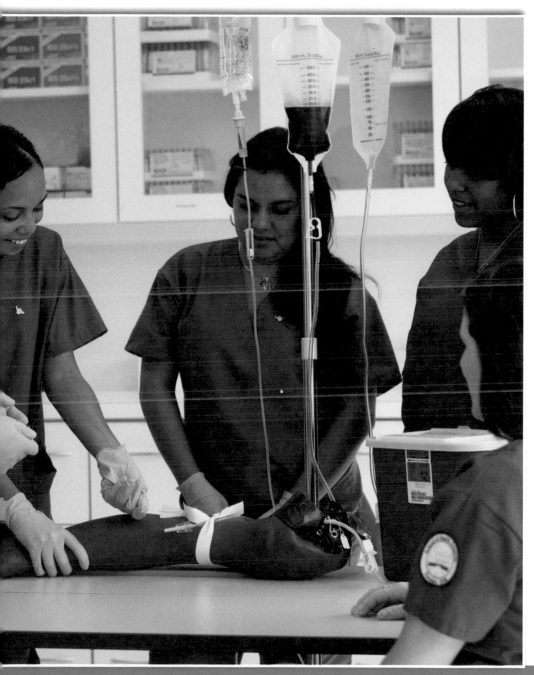

Nurses practice how to properly insert an intravenous (IV) drip at a hospital. Top-notch on-the-job training for new nurses improves job satisfaction rates and promotes better-quality care for patients.

On-the-job training can be a short-term period of less than a month. Highly skilled jobs may require a longer period of a year or more. Entry-level workers with no prior experience will learn the responsibilities and routines of the job. A home health aide, for example, will learn basic medical tasks such as how to properly apply bandages. He or she will also learn standard household duties, such as cooking a nutritious meal for a patient with special dietary considerations. A medical assistant may learn about office procedures or clinical duties, depending on the job description.

Licenses, Certification, and Registration

Before starting to take home a paycheck, a prospective health care worker may have to formally prove his or her qualifications. Many states require that health

A CT scan technician adjusts a patient's position in the machine. Many medical imaging technicians and technologists receive credentials from the American Registry of Radiologic Technologists.

care workers hold a professional license, certificate, or registration. A health care worker's job is a big responsibility. Patients' lives and well-being will be in his or her hands. Since health care workers are required to keep up-to-date with licenses and other credentials, patients can be sure that their health care providers are competent.

As you're preparing to launch your health care career, you must check whether you are required to hold a license or other credentials. If you attended a community college, your academic adviser will be able to give you the details.

Professional licenses are granted directly by states. If a license is required, it is illegal to practice your occupation without a license. Standards vary from one state to another. If you have any questions, you should contact your state government. States generally require that a licensed health care worker hold an associate's degree, certificate, or diploma.

A candidate may also be required to pass a national certification examination as part of the licensing process. These tests are generally drawn up by a national accreditation board for the specific field. Sometimes, there are different levels of accreditation within an occupation. A respiratory therapist, for example, must earn an entry-level credential before becoming eligible to qualify for the advanced exam. In some instances, states may require continuing education in the field for license renewal.

Licenses are not required for some health care occupations, such as home health aide and medical assistant. Nonetheless, workers may choose to pursue certification. Many employers prefer to hire workers who are certified by professional associations. Medical assistants can be certified by the American Association of Medical Assistants or the

American Medical Technologists. Requirements for certification may include receiving a diploma from a community college or the passing of an exam.

Home health aides can receive certification from the National Association for Home Care and Hospice. Candidates must complete seventy-five hours of training, prove competency on the job, and pass an exam. Certification is highly recommended for home aides. Many patients are nervous about the risk of hiring an uncertified aide who could mistreat them or abuse their trust.

CHAPTER THREE

Searching for Health Care Jobs

A job search isn't an easy process. Even in the field of health care, where capable professionals are in high demand, you can get overwhelmed trying to sort out your potential opportunities.

Until you're hired, you should consider the job search your full-time job. Get organized. You should keep records of possible job leads, positions you've applied for, and contact information of professionals in the field. Call up people who may give you a reference, such as former teachers, guidance counselors, supervisors, or colleagues. Keep a checklist of things to do, and don't procrastinate. Spend time every day refining, updating, and expanding your search.

Make sure that you have an appropriate e-mail address for contacting potential employers. Don't use cute or vulgar IDs for your e-mail address (like "PartyGirlPatricia@msn.com"). Instead, keep them serious and straightforward, preferably your actual name or some easily recognizable version of it for professional contacts (like PatriciaCollins@gmail.com or PCollins@gmail.com). If your community college provides you with e-mail service, that's great. An ".edu" suffix on your e-mail address will indicate that you're educated in your field.

As you're searching for a job, try to stay busy with other activities as well. Do some volunteer work, take up a hobby, or offer to help with odd jobs for family and friends. When a

Job seekers should maintain well-organized paper and electronic records in order to keep track of promising leads and the status of job applications. Make a habit of entering daily updates.

job interviewer asks you what you've been doing lately, you'll be able to honestly state that you've been using your time productively and describe exactly how you've been doing so.

Career Resources

There is a wide variety of resources available for job seekers. If you attended a community college, you should take advantage of your school's career services center. It will offer helpful information and strategies for every step of the job search process. Career counselors can offer guidance and answer questions. You can browse job postings from area employers interested in hiring qualified graduates. You may be able to set up an online profile and portfolio through the community college's career services Web site. Career services centers provide many valuable job search tools for free, so don't overlook them.

Public libraries also offer useful job search resources. They often have a separate section of career reference books such as career guides organized by field and books devoted to job search strategies. You can also browse newspapers and periodicals for job listings and information. Some libraries may offer information sessions, workshops, or job help centers. Your library may also offer online resources and databases, not to mention computer terminals and Internet access, that could help you with your job search.

Job fairs provide an opportunity to meet with potential employers. A job fair may be sponsored by your school, the local government, or companies looking to expand their workforce. At a health care job fair, you can talk to recruiters from area health care facilities and staffing agencies. Be sure to dress professionally, and bring copies of your résumé. Show a positive attitude, and don't be shy about talking to the recruiters. In advance, you might want to prepare some questions about the job and an articulate response to "So, tell me about yourself."

Healthcare Staffing

Healthcare Professionals

Advance your career and earn what you deserve.

Immediate Opportunities:

- Nursing
- Diagnostic Imaging
- Clinical Laboratory
- Respiratory Therapy
- Medical Financial
- Physical Therapy

A community college student scans a health care job fair announcement seeking medical workers in a range of career fields.

Other career resources may also be available in your area. Employment services, for example, match employers and potential employees. Some state and local government agencies also offer resources for job seekers.

Looking for Jobs Online

The Internet offers a wealth of tools and information for job seekers. If you enter the term "health care career" into a search engine, you'll receive a long list of sites. Some will be useful; others will offer little practical help. Make sure that the Web sites you visit are reputable before you enter any personal information on them.

▶ ABOUT US

▶ CERTIFICATION

▶ MEMBER SERVICES

▶ CONTINUING EDUCATION

▶ MEETINGS & EVENTS

▶ SCHOOLS & STUDENTS

▶ EMPLOYERS

Certifying Excelle

Welcome to AMT!

Check out our latest additions to our On-Demand CE Courses. 7 newly added courses (Click Here).

American Medical Technologists (AMT) is a nonprofit and professional membership association representi individuals in allied health care. Established in 1939, providing allied health professionals with professiona services and membership programs to enhance thei personal growth. Upon certification, individuals auto

Professional associations, such as American Medical Technologists (www.americanmedtech .org), offer a range of valuable services to job seekers and established professionals alike.

There are many career sites that list job openings. Some specialize in health care jobs. Others are large, general career sites that list health care careers as only one category among

SEARCH

0 Item(s) In Cart   Total: $0.0(

& ADVOCACY | CONTACT US | LOG]

Members Log In To:

Pay Dues Online
Check Certification
Submit CEUs
Update Your Profile

Log In Now

Health

News
G-2 Lab Institute Report 2012
Read More

ADVANCE Partners with
American Medical Technologists
Read More

hundreds. You can generally enter your location to find jobs available in your region. Many newspapers also post job openings online. Check out the job listings published in your local paper. These may be more likely than the big jobs sites to include help-wanted ads by smaller local employers. Sometimes there are alternate job titles for the same occupation. For example, if you're looking for a job as a home health aide, check out listings for "home attendant," and "home support worker" as well.

There are professional societies for many health care specialties. For example, the American Medical Technologists offers certification for a number of specialties, including medical assistant. The organization also provides networking and career services. If you're not sure whether there's a relevant professional society for your specialty, check with a career counselor. The BLS *Occupational Outlook Handbook* also provides such information.

Finally, check out the Web sites for local health care facilities and staffing agencies, which usually list job openings under a heading like "Careers."

Using Connections and Networking

Chances are, you're surrounded by family, friends, colleagues, and casual acquaintances who would be very happy to help you get a good job if they are in a position to do so. This is your network. As your career advances, you will develop a broader professional network within your field of employment.

But even if you're still developing your network, the people around you might be able to help out. Maybe a former volunteer supervisor at a hospital knows about a nursing home that needs to hire medical assistants. Perhaps one of your former classmates heard that her employer was planning to expand its workforce. If nothing else, the people around you might be able to offer good career tips and advice based on their own experiences. Listen to them and promptly follow up on any promising leads.

You should do your own footwork, too, as you're hunting for a job. A health care company in your area might not list any current job openings on its Web site. But you'd love to work for that company. You should pay the facility a visit in person and stop by its human resources department. Do your best to make a good impression—dress professionally and be courteous to everyone. Drop off a copy of your résumé at the human resources department and introduce yourself. If someone in the department considers you a good candidate, he or she might remember you when a job opens up.

Drafting the Perfect Résumé

A résumé is a document that summarizes your professional qualifications. It includes education and work experience. It

COVER LETTERS

The cover letter is an important element of a job application. A cover letter should be addressed to your prospective employer. Its purpose is to introduce yourself. Your cover letter should demonstrate your written communication skills and get across a sense of your personality. Be sure to maintain a professional tone throughout, however. You might reiterate some of the important points from your résumé, but don't just summarize your résumé in the cover letter. An effective cover letter can grab your prospective interviewer's attention and make you stand out from the rest of the applicants. A poorly written cover letter can sabotage your chances of obtaining an interview. Unless the employer specifies "no cover letters," you should include one in applications and with résumés sent online or by conventional mail.

also lists other relevant information such as extracurricular and volunteer activities, awards, credentials, interests, or skills that might be pertinent to the job. Your résumé presents your accomplishments to potential employers before they ever meet you. A solid résumé can create a good initial impression.

There are many different formats for résumés, but most include the same basic layout. Your name and contact information is listed at the top. The body of the document includes your educational background, your work experience, and additional pertinent information. When possible, you should tailor your résumé to the position you're applying for. If you're applying to work as a nursing assistant at a nursing home,

Job seekers applying for a position should submit a résumé or a curriculum vitae (CV). A CV includes a longer summary of educational background and professional experience than a résumé.

emphasize your volunteer work at a hospital. If you're applying for a medical assistant job in an office, emphasize your customer service work at a summer job.

If you have never drafted a résumé before, you should probably consult books and Web sites for tips. Then you should ask a career counselor to review your document. It's very important to avoid typos and inconsistent formatting. The counselor may also have suggestions about the sort of information that you should add, delete, emphasize, or de-emphasize.

CHAPTER FOUR

Preparing for Testing and Job Interviews

The night before your job interview or professional certification exam, you'll be nervous. It's natural to feel jittery before such an important occasion. But you should also go in with a feeling of confidence because the best approach is to prepare well in advance.

If you're about to take a certification exam, you should study weeks beforehand. Your education or training will have familiarized you with all of the material. If you spend plenty of time reviewing your subjects well before the exam, you should be in good shape to receive a passing score.

If you're about to attend a job interview, you should have a checklist prepared well in advance so that you won't have any last-minute panic attacks. There's one preliminary step you should take as soon as you launch your job search: assessing your wardrobe. Do you have a nice suit or a few appropriate outfits to wear to job interviews? If not, go shopping for some professional clothes. Another important step is to assemble a list of references for potential employers.

Preparing for a Test

You need to start your test preparation significantly in advance of your target test date. Visit the Web site of the

Prepare thoroughly ahead of time for a certification test by studying and familiarizing yourself with the format. This will boost your confidence as well as improve your grasp of the material.

certification board or professional association that administers the test. When do you need to register to take the exam? The American Association of Medical Assistants, for example, requires that certification applicants register and pay a fee at least three months in advance. You should review the qualification requirements and compile any necessary paperwork, such as school transcripts, necessary for your application.

The certification board or professional association Web site will also provide you with plenty of relevant information on the test itself. You should learn everything you can about

Good study habits are key to preparing for an important exam. Instead of just memorizing facts and figures, make sure that you understand all the concepts relevant to the subject matter.

the format of the exam and the testing procedures. Review the length of the test and type of questions. Is the exam timed? What topics are covered? The site may provide review materials and practice tests. If you have any questions, go ahead and send an e-mail to the organization.

In addition, you should review various general test preparation strategies. Take a highlighter to your review sheets and mark any particularly thorny topics. Look online for additional study materials. Study in a group if your classmates are also preparing for the test. Take plenty of practice tests, but remember that each test is just a sampling of the entire body of material. It won't prepare you for everything that will be on the test or exactly what will be on the test. Talk to someone who has passed the exam and ask for additional tips.

When you schedule the exam, you will probably choose the closest testing center in your area. If you have to take a long trip, you might want to stay in a nearby hotel the night before. You will receive an information packet when your test date is confirmed. Check the testing time and the arrival time. It will include a list of what to bring, such as a legal ID and confirmation materials. The night before the exam, try to get a good night's rest. In the morning, allow for plenty of extra travel time in case you get delayed.

Preparing for an Interview

You should start general job interview preparations well before you make your first interview appointment. You don't want to realize the day before the interview that you haven't made a list of references and that you don't have anything to wear.

It's important to make a positive first impression on a prospective employer by dressing professionally. Shop for business-appropriate clothes if you don't already have them. Regardless of your qualifications, the first thing your interviewer notices is your appearance and attitude.

References are people whom potential employers contact about your work performance. A glowing report from a well-respected member of the industry can be a powerful asset to your job search. Think carefully about whom you want to ask to provide references. Former colleagues, professors, and supervisors are a good choice. Your references should be working professionals. Friends and family members are not appropriate as work references.

Your clothes and personal appearance can contribute to a positive first impression. If you don't have any professional clothing appropriate for the interview, go out and buy some. Men should wear a suit, tie, and dress shoes. Women have a

FINDING A MENTOR

A mentor can be a valuable source of support as you're starting out on the path toward a career in health care. A mentor is an experienced professional in your field who can listen to your concerns and offer guidance. He or she can also help you with networking and understanding health care bureaucracy. You may consider your mentor a friend, even a close friend. But the relationship is often more formal and respectful than your friendship with peers.

You might find your mentor through a job, volunteer work, mutual acquaintances, or your parents and their friends. In addition, colleges and professional associations have mentoring programs that connect new workers in a field to mentors willing to share their insights.

greater variety of options, which can make the choice more difficult. In general, pick out an outfit that is more formal and conservative than regular workplace attire. You want your interviewer to remember your professional qualifications, not your lime-green tank top. Try out a business suit, or pants or a skirt in black or a neutral color paired with a nice blouse. Buy several combinations that you can mix and match. Jeans, sneakers, flip-flops, and bare shoulders are never appropriate for an interview.

You may schedule or confirm your interview over the phone. This preliminary contact is your first chance to demonstrate your professionalism. Try to be calm and courteous. Once you've made the appointment, do some background research on your potential employer. Look at the company's Web site and take notes. When was the company started?

What is its primary focus? How is it structured? Does it have a news section describing recent projects, programs, achievements, and activities? Compile a list of informed questions about the workplace and potential job. Also, make note of any details that you find particularly interesting. It will make a good impression if you can show genuine enthusiasm about the prospect of working at the company.

Do an interview rehearsal ahead of time. Have a friend ask you questions that you think might come up during your interview. A mock interview will give you a chance to practice giving articulate answers and presenting yourself as a qualified professional.

Getting Organized Ahead of Time

The day before your appointment, you should assemble everything you'll need for the interview. Lay out your clothes and make sure that everything is clean and wrinkle-free. Pay attention to details. Nail polish is fine as long as it's subtle, for example. Chipped nail polish, however, might create a bad impression. Tattoos should be covered if possible and most piercings removed. It's a good idea to take extra care with your personal appearance before a job interview.

You should also assemble all of your professional materials. Print out extra copies of your cover letter, résumé, and references. You may want to take along proof of professional certification or a portfolio of college course work that demonstrates your abilities. Make sure that you have the name and contact information for your interviewer at hand. You don't want to have to tell the receptionist that you have an appointment with "what's-his-name." Print out an interview schedule if relevant.

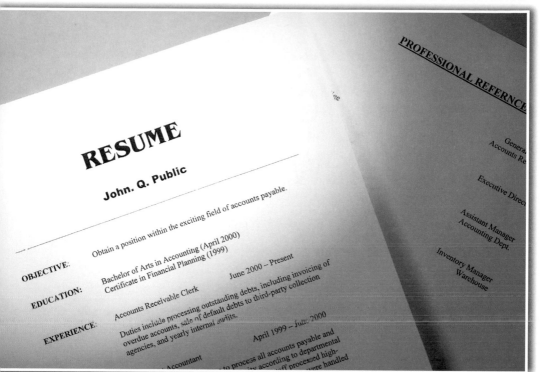

Take along extra copies of your résumé to the job interview. If more than one person attends the interview, you'll be able to hand out extras and demonstrate that you're organized and prepared for contingencies.

It is critically important that you arrive to the interview ahead of your appointment time. Punctuality demonstrates that you have a good work ethic. If you're unfamiliar with the area, map out your route ahead of time. You may even want to do a test drive to the location. Print out a map and directions if you're at all uncertain. In addition, some hospitals and office buildings are huge and have a confusing layout. If so, allow for extra time to find your interviewer's office.

CHAPTER FIVE

Acing Your Job Interview

You should go into a job interview well-prepared, with a positive attitude. Of course you'll be nervous. But if you've done a thorough job of getting ready for the big day, you'll feel a sense of confidence about your prospects. Get a good night's sleep before your interview and don't skip breakfast. If you're tired or embarrassed by a growling stomach, you're more likely to be distracted during the interview and not as sharp as you should be.

Be yourself—the interviewer will recognize sincerity and real enthusiasm. Don't just parrot pat and rote answers or say what you think people want to hear. Show some individual and critical intelligence and personality. But convey a professional persona, too. Don't act too casual. The interviewer is a potential boss and colleague, not a potential friend. If you're relatively new to the workplace, don't be afraid to admit it. Your interviewer will be more impressed by honesty and a willingness and ability to learn and work hard than by exaggerated claims about work experience.

What to Expect

The most common type of job interview is the one-on-one interview with a hiring manager or someone from the human

On the day of the interview, allow extra time for travel in case you experience delays beyond your control, such as a train running late, slow traffic, or difficulty finding parking.

resources department. But there are other formats that you should be prepared for. Sometimes a prospective employee attends a succession of interviews with different management figures during the visit. An interview may be held on the phone or over a video connection. In group interviews, several people might jointly interview a single candidate. Conversely, one person might interview several candidates simultaneously or in quick succession. Most of the time, the interview takes place in a workplace setting, such as an office or conference room. Sometimes, however, an interview might be held at a restaurant or cafe.

Some employers require that candidates take a pre-employment personality test. The results are intended to serve as an indicator of your likely job performance. You may also be taken on a tour of the premises during your appointment or be introduced to other personnel.

The bulk of the interview is your opportunity to make a sales pitch on why you're the best candidate for the job. If the interviewer opens with "Tell me about yourself," you should reply with a brief description of your professional and educational history. Add a brief relevant anecdote or mention an exceptional skill that might make you stand out from other candidates.

When discussing your background, emphasize why your education and work experiences match the job requirements. Give specific answers that illustrate your strengths rather than vague answers that aren't connected to your qualifications. Instead of telling the interviewer random trivia about yourself, focus on accomplishments and achievements.

Expect to undergo multiple rounds of interviews. If you made a favorable impression during your initial interview,

Demonstrate a positive attitude in order to convince the employer that you'd be a good person to work with on a day-to-day basis. Smile, make eye contact, and be positive and courteous.

the next step will be a callback. Even when they've decided to make you a job offer, you may go through one final interview.

Top Ten Things Not to Say in an Interview

- "I don't have any weaknesses." Often, an interviewer will ask a candidate about weaknesses or past failures. One good possible answer is to discuss a weakness that you've taken steps to correct. For example, you could say that because you don't feel that you're naturally technically adept, you've taken extra computer classes.
- "I have no idea what I'll be doing in five years." Interviewers sometimes ask about the long-term future to learn about a candidate's goals and ambitions. A possible answer would be to describe how, if you got the job, you'd be interested in pursuing further training in the field that would lead to advancement.
- Negative statements about former employers. Overall, you want to remain positive during your interview. Try to find something favorable or at least neutral to say when discussing past work experiences. The interviewer probably won't be interested in a hiring a candidate who freely bad-mouths the boss.
- "Sorry about that, let me turn off my phone…" Turn off your cell phone before walking into the interview. Never take a call while being interviewed.
- Interruptions of any sort. Wait for the interviewer to finish the question. Give it a brief moment of thought before replying.

- "Let me tell you a little more about that one time that…" Answer questions completely, but don't talk too much. Keep your focus on your professional qualifications and abilities.
- Lies. Don't exaggerate your accomplishments. Even if you're not caught, you're less likely to succeed in the job if you misrepresent your abilities.
- "Er, well…" "Like, you know…" "Um…" It's not easy to be poised and articulate, especially when you are nervous. Doing mock interviews ahead of time will help you compose your thoughts as you speak. Don't rush into answers. You might want to take along some notes jotted down ahead of time in case you completely blank out on a response.

WATCHING YOUR (BODY) LANGUAGE

You might be surprised to learn that even if you're articulate and composed for the interview, your body language might be undermining your good impression. Body language is what we communicate with our physical postures and gestures. Some elements of body language are obvious blunders. You shouldn't slouch in your chair, for example, or sit with your arms crossed defensively. Make a note of positive body language signals that you can achieve. Shake hands firmly when you greet the interviewer. Make and maintain eye contact to show that you're engaged. Don't forget to smile no matter how nervous you are. Be relaxed, but sit up straight and don't fidget, touch your face, or fiddle with your hair.

• "I don't have any questions." If the interviewer asks if you have any questions, use it as an opportunity to show that you're engaged and well-informed about the company.
• "I really need this job because I'm broke." Your goal is to convince the company that they need you, not to tell them about your own needs. In addition, you should focus on your professional background. Your personal circumstances generally aren't relevant to your merits as a potential employee.

Top Ten Things You Should Talk About in an Interview

• Specific reasons you're interested in working for the employer.
• Factors that initially attracted you to the field of health care. Be honest—it's probably a combination of practical reasons such as job security as well as a desire to help others.
• Examples of instances when you've successfully worked as part of a team. Also examples where you've shown individual initiative.
• Strengths and qualifications that set you above the general pool of applicants.
• A situation that you resolved through problem-solving skills.
• Realistic expectations. Health care can be a demanding field. Acknowledge that you recognize some of the difficult aspects of your specialty. Talk about reasons you consider yourself up for the job.

At the end of the interview, ask about the next stage of the hiring process and reiterate your enthusiasm for the position. Don't forget to smile and thank the interviewer for his or her time.

- Transferable skills, especially ones that you didn't list in your résumé. Do you speak Spanish? Are you familiar with accounting software? Either could be useful in a hospital setting.
- Your willingness to learn and achieve if you get the job.
- Your techniques for dealing with stress and how they'd enable you to thrive if you got the job.
- "Thank-you." Courteous behavior is important throughout the interview. In particular, be sure to thank the interviewer when the interview is concluded.

Soon after the interview, write a thank-you e-mail or letter to the interviewers in order to express your appreciation for being considered for the job and to remind them that you'd be a great and qualified employee.

After the Interview

You might be tempted to kick back and celebrate after a promising job interview. If you really want the job, however, you should immediately follow up by writing a thank-you note to the interviewer. Restate your case that you're the best applicant for the job. If relevant, build on or clarify some of the points that arose during the interview. Mention that the more you learn about the employer, the more interested you are in joining the company. In most cases, a follow-up, thank-you e-mail is as effective as a letter sent by conventional mail.

If you haven't heard back within a few days, make a follow-up call. Politely remind your interviewer who your are and ask if the position has been filled. Reiterate your interest in the job. Don't call back multiple times, however—it will not help your chances of employment. And even if you aren't hired, the employer may keep your résumé on file for future openings if you made a good impression.

In the meantime, keep up your job search. Assess your interview performance. Were you able to communicate your qualifications effectively? Were there any questions that you found particularly difficult to answer? If you don't receive a job offer, don't get discouraged. Learn from your mistakes in order to improve your showing in the next interview.

CHAPTER SIX

The First Day of Your New Career

Sooner or later, your job search will pay off with a job offer and your new boss saying, "So we'll see you on Monday!" You'll probably be nervous about walking into the workplace for the first time as an employee. And it is a big milestone in your professional life. If you make a good first impression and establish yourself as a dependable worker with a positive attitude, it will be a great kickoff for your future career.

You should do more than get a good sleep the night before—you should establish a healthy sleep schedule well in advance of your first day. That way, you'll be accustomed to getting up and out, alert and ready for morning activities. You should also take particular care with your appearance and work preparation on your first day. You don't want the new colleagues you're meeting for the first time to think of you as the girl with the wrinkled shirt or the guy jotting reminders on the back of one hand.

Getting Started

On your first day of work, you will have to pay special attention to everything going on around you. You'll be introduced to your coworkers and superiors. Someone will show you around and describe your daily schedule. You will probably

On the first day of work, a new employee will meet coworkers in the same field, as well as specialists in a variety of areas who collaborate on patient care.

have a break for lunch as well as a couple of other short breaks throughout the day. Perhaps you will receive your work uniforms, or you'll put in an order for one in your size. You'll settle into your designated workspace and learn the workplace rules and routines. By the end of the day, you might end up with a whole stack of paperwork on company policies and procedures. In addition, you should take notes on key points that you specifically want to remember. If you don't understand something, ask for clarification. It could save you confusion later on.

You will probably also have a meeting with someone in the human resources department where you will fill out new hire paperwork. At this point, you will also review the details of your benefits. The company may offer, for example, health insurance, paid vacation time, and a retirement plan. You may have choices to make on some points of your benefits package.

Settling In

You'll quickly grow accustomed to the atmosphere of your workplace, whether it's a busy hospital, an orderly laboratory, a pharmacy in a strip mall, or a private dentist's office. You will learn your specific duties as you receive job training and gradually start taking on more responsibilities. Learn from the example of your coworkers. If someone offers constructive criticism, accept it gratefully and gracefully. It will take a while for you to fully recognize all of the subtleties of appropriate workplace conduct.

In some cases, you may spend most of your days away from the main office. Most home health aides, for example, work for a home health care agency that provides staffing to clients. If you are hired by the agency, you will first undergo a training period. You'll learn about giving medical and personal care. In addition, you'll learn how to become integrated as part of a team that includes nurses and various doctors and is charged with providing patients' medical care. Your supervisor will also emphasize that you are a guest in someone's home and that you should treat the home and your client with the utmost respect.

Being a Great Employee

Once you've finished your training and have learned the routines at your workplace, you can begin concentrating on

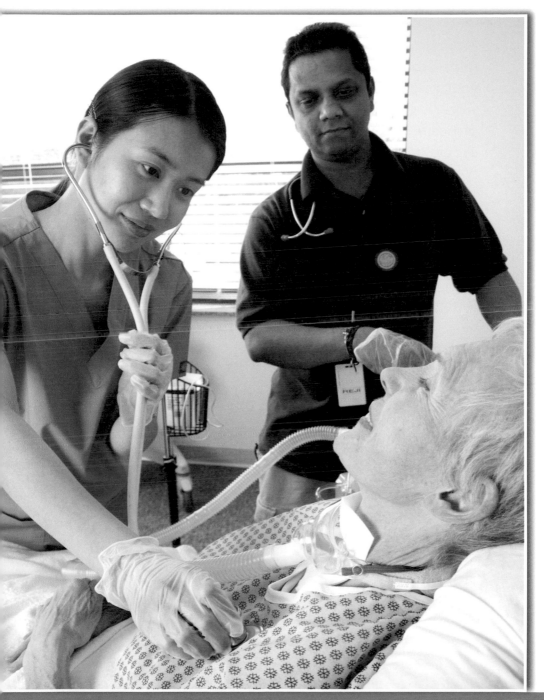

A nurse and a pulmonary technician care for a patient experiencing a lung ailment. Teamwork is vital in health care, since each team member brings specialized abilities to the diagnostic and treatment process.

maintaining a good work ethic. That means that you are committed to forming good habits on the job. You stay focused on your responsibilities. You pay attention to the quality of your work. A good work ethic is particularly important in the field of health care. A health care job is a position of trust. You should be aware of patient confidentiality and the sensitivity of patients' medical records.

No matter how much you work to demonstrate professional behavior in the workplace, there's a chance that conflict could arise with one of your coworkers. If that happens, don't let it interfere with your job performance. Try to resolve your differences politely or discuss the situation with your supervisor.

MANAGING YOUR MONEY

Now that you're earning a steady paycheck, it's time to go out on a big shopping spree, right? Not so fast. You deserve to celebrate your achievement, but you should also mark your financial independence by establishing responsible money management practices. Don't spend more money than you earn. If you need to take out a loan for a big purchase, discuss it with a financial planner at a bank first. Set up a budget for your spending. Allot a certain amount each month to categories such as rent, utilities, living expenses, transportation, entertainment, and savings. Consider long-term financial goals as well as short-term needs. Also, set aside a certain amount of money that you can access easily in case of emergency.

Your Long-Term Career Path

Periodically, you will receive informal or formal feedback on your job. An example of informal feedback would be a word of praise from your boss for some of your work. An example of formal feedback is your annual performance review. Generally, you are assessed on how well you have met expectations in a number of categories. If you receive a favorable performance review, it could bring with it a promotion or a pay increase. Part of your review will include a self-evaluation. You'll also set goals for the next year.

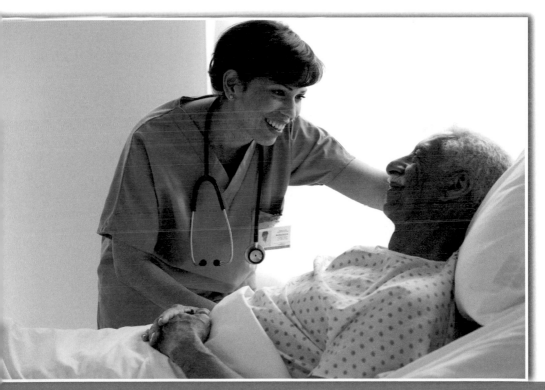

A nurse offers physical and emotional support to a patient. As entry-level workers gain job experience in health care, they will come to recognize particular strengths, weaknesses, and interests that may shape their future pursuits in the field.

Entry-level health care careers provide a good foundation for future advancement in the field. Many hospitals and staffing agencies offer continuing education. A medical assistant may undergo further education or training and become a specialized technician. Or a medical assistant may take business classes and become an office manager. A home health aide could study to become a nursing aide or even a registered nurse. It can be highly beneficial for the staffing agency to encourage quality workers to take on more responsibilities. Your supervisor will already know that you'd continue to do good work for the company as a nurse.

Remember that the field of health care can offer great flexibility. If you decide that you'd like to try a slower-paced workplace than a big hospital, you might be able to get a job at a rehabilitation clinic. If you want to make a sudden move across the country for personal reasons, you probably won't have much trouble landing a job quickly. The job market is thriving for health care, especially once you establish yourself as a professional in the field with credentials and a solid work background.

analytic Separating something into component parts or constituent elements; skilled in thinking or reasoning.

associate's degree An undergraduate degree generally awarded after two years of study.

career counselor A counselor who helps guide people through the processes of beginning, developing, or changing careers.

certification The awarding of a certificate upon completion of a course of study or passing of an exam.

chronic Long in duration, as in a disease.

credential Proof, usually written, that demonstrates someone's identity, authority, or qualifications.

diagnose To identify the nature of a medical condition by examining the symptoms.

examination In medicine, a physical inspection of the patient's body performed in order to assess health.

hygiene Practices that promote good health and prevent disease, especially cleanliness.

license Official permission from the government or other authority, such as to practice a trade.

occupational therapy Therapy intended to help people better perform tasks in their everyday work and personal lives.

portfolio A representative sampling of work that displays someone's accomplishments or abilities.

qualification A condition or standard that must be complied with (as for the attainment of a privilege or a job); a quality or skill that makes one suitable for a job.

reference Someone providing a statement of professional qualifications regarding a job applicant; also, the statement itself.

rehabilitation Restoring or returning someone to a healthy condition.

résumé A summary of one's professional qualifications and work experience.

technician Someone trained in practical application and knowledge, especially of a mechanical or scientific subject.

technologist Someone trained in principles and practical applications, especially of a mechanical or scientific subject. A technologist has a higher education level than a technician.

vital signs Clinical measurements, such as body temperature and blood pressure, that indicate a patient's general physical condition.

volunteer To take part in unpaid work of one's own free will.

American Association of Medical Assistants (AAMA)
20 North Wacker Drive, Suite 1575
Chicago, IL 60606
(312) 899-1500
Web site: http://aama-ntl.org
The AAMA is the professional association for medical
  assistants that provides certification and other services.

American Medical Association (AMA)
515 North State Street
Chicago, IL 60654
(800) 621-8335
Web site: http://www.ama-assn.org
The professional organization for physicians, the AMA also
  provides useful information for a variety of health care
  subfields.

American Medical Technologists (AMT)
10700 West Higgins Road, Suite 150
Rosemont IL, 60018
(847) 823-5169
Web site: http://www.americanmedtech.org
The AMT is the certification agency and membership
  society that provides services for a number of allied
  health profession specialties.

American Occupational Therapy Association (AOTA)
4720 Montgomery Lane
Bethesda, MD 20814
(301) 652-2682
Web site: http://www.aota.org

The AOTA is the association that provides certification and other services to professionals and students in the field of occupational therapy.

Canadian Medical Association (CMA)
1867 Alta Vista Drive
Ottawa, ON K1G 5W8
Canada
(888) 855-2555
Web site: http://www.cma.ca
The CMA is the association of physicians that advocates on the behalf of its members and the public.

Commission on Accreditation of Allied Health Educational Programs (CAAHEP)
1361 Park Street
Clearwater, FL 33756
(727) 210-2350
Web site: http://www.caahep.org
The CAAHEP provides accreditation to educational programs in health science professions. In addition, it offers information for students on accredited programs.

National Association for Home Care and Hospice (NAHC)
228 Seventh Street SE
Washington, DC 20003
(202) 547-7424
Web site: http://nahc.org
The NAHC is a trade association representing the interests and concerns of home care agencies, hospices, and home care aide organizations. It also provides certification and accreditation programs for members.

Service Canada: Job Bank
Human Resources and Skills Development Canada
355 North River Road
Place Vanier, Tower B, 8th floor, Mail Stop VB801
Ottawa, ON K1A 0L1
Canada
Web site: http://www.jobbank.gc.ca
Job Bank is Canada's government-run jobs-listing Web site
    that connects job seekers and employers.

Web Sites

Due to the changing nature of Internet links, Rosen Publishing has developed an online list of Web sites related to the subject of this book. This site is updated regularly. Please use this link to access the list:

http://www.rosenlinks.com/JOBS/Health

American Library Association editors. *How to Get a Great Job*. New York, NY: Skyhorse Publishing, 2011.

Barker, Geoff. *Health and Social Care Careers*. Mankato, MN: AMICUS, 2011.

Bennington, Emily, and Skip Lineberg. *Effective Immediately: How to Fit In, Stand Out, and Move Up at Your First Real Job*. Berkeley, CA: Ten Speed Press, 2010.

Beshara, Tony. *Acing the Interview: How to Ask and Answer the Questions That Will Get You the Job*. New York, NY: AMACOM, 2008.

Bolles, Richard N. *The Job-Hunter's Survival Guide: How to Find Hope and Rewarding Work, Even When "There Are No Jobs."* Berkeley, CA: Ten Speed Press, 2009.

Farr, Michael. *The Quick Resume and Cover Letter Book: Write and Use an Effective Resume in Only One Day*. Indianapolis, IN: JIST Works, 2011.

Ferguson. *Medical Technicians and Technologists* (Careers in Focus). New York, NY: Ferguson, 2009.

Ferguson. *The Top 100: The Fastest-Growing Careers for the 21st Century*. 5th ed. New York, NY: Facts On File, 2011.

Field, Shelly. *Career Opportunities in Health Care*. New York, NY: Ferguson, 2007.

Holland, R. William. *Cracking the New Job Market: The 7 Rules for Getting Hired in Any Economy*. New York, NY: AMACOM, 2012.

Kimball, Cheryl. *Start Your Health Care Career*. Irvine, CA: Entrepreneur Press, 2007.

Long, Landon, and Jesse Stretch. *The Unspoken Rules of Getting Hired: 107 Job Hunting Secrets That Employers Do Not Want You to Know*. North Charleston, SC: BookSurge Publishing, 2012.

MacDougall, Debra Angel, and Elisabeth Harney Sanders-Park. *The 6 Reasons You'll Get the Job: What Employers Look for—Whether They Know It or Not.* New York, NY: Prentice Hall Press, 2010.

McGraw-Hill editors. *The Big Book of Jobs.* New York, NY: McGraw-Hill, 2011.

Shatkin, Laurence, and Michael Farr. *Top 100 Careers Without a Four-Year Degree.* Indianapolis, IN: JIST Works, 2012.

Stevens, Peggy Noe. *Professional Presence: A Four-Part Program for Building Your Personal Brand.* Austin, TX: Greenleaf Book Group Press, 2012.

Stratford, S.J. *Ferguson Field Guides to Finding a New Career: Health Care.* New York, NY: Checkmark Books, 2009.

Weeks, Zona R. *Opportunities in Occupational Therapy Careers.* New York, NY: McGraw Hill, 2007.

Wischnitzer, Saul, and Edith Wischnitzer. *Top 100 Health-Care Careers: Your Complete Guidebook to Training and Jobs in Allied Health, Nursing, Medicine, and More.* 3rd ed. Indianapolis, IN: JIST Works, 2011.

Yate, Martin. *Knock 'em Dead: The Ultimate Job Search Guide.* Avon, MA: Adams Media, 2011.

BIBLIOGRAPHY

American Medical Association. *Health Care Careers Directory 2011–2012*. 39th ed. Chicago, IL: American Medical Association, 2011.

Bureau of Labor Statistics. *Occupational Outlook Handbook, 2012*. Retrieved October 2012 (http://www.bls.gov/ooh).

Damp, Dennis V. *Health Care Job Explosion! High Growth Health Care Careers and Job Locators*. McKees Rocks, PA: Bookhaven Press, 2006.

Kacen, Alex. *Opportunities in Allied Health Careers*. New York, NY: McGraw-Hill, 2005.

New York Times. "The New Old Age: Caring and Coping." Retrieved October 2012 (http://newoldage.blogs .nytimes.com).

Reeves, Ellen Gordon. *Can I Wear My Nose Ring to the Interview? The Crash Course in Finding, Landing, and Keeping Your First Real Job*. New York, NY: Workman Publishing, 2009.

Torpey, Elka. "High Wages After High School—Without a Bachelor's Degree." *Occupational Outlook Quarterly*, 2012. Retrieved October 2012 (http://www.bls.gov/opub/ooq/ 2012/summer/art03.pdf).

VGM editors. *Resumes for Health and Medical Careers*. 3rd ed. Chicago, IL: VGM Career Books, 2004.

Zedlitz, Robert H. *How to Get a Job in Health Care*. Clifton Park, NY: Delmar Learning, 2003.

INDEX

A

acupuncture, 11
allied health, 4, 10
alternative medicine, 10–11
American Association of
Medical Assistants, 32, 45
American Medical Association,
10, 23
American Medical
Technologists, 33, 39
apprenticeships, 28
associate's degree, 6, 7, 10, 11,
12, 26, 27, 32

B

bachelor's degree, 22, 26
Bureau of Labor Statistics, 5 6,
26, 39

C

chiropractic care, 11
college, 10, 22, 24, 26, 49, 50
communication sciences, 10
community college, 4, 6, 8, 11,
15, 19, 22, 23, 24, 26–28,
32, 33, 34, 36
counseling, 11
cover letters, 41, 50
creative therapy, 8–10, 11

D

dental assistants, 11, 24
dental hygienists, 11, 26
dentistry, 10, 11
diagnostic medical
sonographers, 26
dietetics, 11

E

electroneurodiagnostic (END)
technologist, 8, 10
extracurricular activities,
23–24, 41

G

geriatric population, 17, 19

H

health care careers,
advantages of, 15–17
challenges of, 17–18
education, 4, 6, 7, 8, 10, 11,
12, 13, 15, 18, 19, 22–28,
32, 33, 68
entry-level jobs, 6, 18–21, 30, 68
licensing, registering, and
certification, 6, 30–33, 39,
44–47
long-term career plans, 67–68

on-the-job training, 4, 7, 13, 15, 28–30
outlook for field, 6
schedule, 17
testing for, 32, 33, 44–47
types of, 10–15
Health Care Careers Directory, 23
health information and communication field, 5, 11, 24
health technician, 7, 11
high school, 4, 7, 15, 18
courses to take for a health
care job, 22–26
home health aide, 19, 30, 32, 33, 39, 64, 68

I

interviewing, 35, 44, 47–50
and body language, 57
following up, 60–61
interview do's, 58–59
interview don'ts, 56–58
preparing for, 50–51
typical interview format, 52–56

J

job, new,
first day at work, 62–64
how to be a good employee, 64–66
learning your duties, 64
job searches
career resources, 36–37

networking, 40
online, 37–49

L

laboratory science, 11
licensed practical nurse (LPN), 13
licensed vocational nurse
(LVN), 13
long-term care facilities, 17, 40, 41

M

massage therapy, 11
medical assistant, 7, 10, 18,
19–21, 24, 30, 32, 39, 43, 68
medical imaging, 5, 12
medical transcriptionist, 11
mentors, 49
money management, 66

N

National Association for Home
Care and Hospice, 33
nuclear medicine technologist, 26
nursing, 4, 7, 13, 17, 19, 24, 26,
28, 41, 64, 68

O

*Occupational Outlook
Handbook*, 5–6, 39
online courses, 27

P

personal care aide, 19
pharmacy jobs, 13, 18, 24
physician assistants, 13
podiatry, 13, 21
psychology and psychiatry, 13, 17, 23

R

radiation therapy, 12, 26
radiologic technologist, 26
references, 34, 48, 50
registered nurse (RN), 13, 26, 68
rehabilitation and therapy jobs, 5, 15, 17, 24, 26
respiratory therapist, 10, 26, 32

résumés, 24, 40–43, 50, 59, 61

S

salary, 6, 66, 67
surgical technologist, 10

V

veterinary medicine, 15
vision professions, 15, 18
vocational-technical programs, 4, 24–26
volunteering, 23, 34, 41, 43

X

X-rays, 12

About the Author

Corona Brezina is an author who has written over a dozen young adult books for Rosen Publishing. Several of her previous books have also focused on in-demand careers, including *Careers in Forensics: Medical Examiner* and *Essential Careers: Careers in Meteorology*. She lives in Chicago, Illinois.

Photo Credits